THE CASE OF
SENSATIONAL
STIMS

ERIN GARCIA

ILLUSTRATED BY CHRISTIAN BAJUSZ

Dedicated to our neurodivergent friends and their allies who seek to understand and support them.

And in honor of those who were, or are, currently harmed because of their sensory needs. We love you and are creating a more educated and empathetic world.

When you see a magnifying glass like this 🔍 *on a page, it means there's an additional clue to help our characters solve the mystery. To read more about the clue, turn to pages 26 and 27.*

Hi! My name is Joey. I'm seven and love to play. I'm going to be an animal expert. I'm also autistic, which is awesome.

This means I experience the world in a unique way.

My senses are extra sensitive. I notice many details that others might not. That's one of the coolest things about autism. These details I notice are called sensory input. They make me feel many strong emotions and stimming helps me release them.

Stimming is when I use my body instead of my words to express my feelings.

If I try to stop my stims from happening I can experience sensory overload. This is when all my feelings get trapped inside and I feel like I'll burst! My body just knows when I need to stim.

Loud noises hurt my whole body, not just my ears. When noise is really bothering me, I usually flap my hands.

But I also flap my hands when I'm happy. Stims can look similar, but mean different things.

Stimming makes me feel happy and safe. This is different for my sister, Elise. When she's concentrating, she twirls her hair but stops when she wants. She manages her feelings differently. That's just the way she is. I don't need to twirl my hair when I focus.

Anyway, hippopotamuses are my passion. I love them! I'm writing hippo facts, then playing with Elise. We have so much fun!

Mom bought me a hippo book and a new lamp to read it by. I'm all set!

Joey! I need your help! I can't solve this puzzle and you're so good at them. Wait — why is Joey doing an upset stim?!

It's so loud! I need help but I can't seem to explain what I need!

Joey's upset! He has his hippo book and a new light. He should be happy! This is a mystery. To help my brother, I must use my senses— like my eyes, and my ears, but most of all, **my heart.**

Even though he's upset, Joey is safe. I can help him while mom cooks dinner. But why is he upset? I'm on the case!

Why isn't Joey reading his new book? Hippos are his favorite.

He likes them even more than blue iguanas.

Even more than pangolins.

Even more than **RING-TAILED LEMURS!**

It's almost dinner! I need another clue to solve this case. He's flapping his hands. **That happens when there's lots of noise.**

That sound! I feel awful! I can't explain it. I don't want to disappoint Elise and I want to finish my hippo facts! **I am overwhelmed.**

Hmmm... Joey has moved away from his book and new light...

Oh my!

The lamp is buzzing. I didn't hear it at first, but now it's bugging me too! Let's turn it off. There. **The buzzing is gone!**

You couldn't hear that?!

It's explosive!!!

Hmm... why would it be buzzing? Wait! Mom's using the microwave! In science we learned that when certain lights are on at the same time as an appliance, buzzing can happen. It's called **electromagnetic interference.**

Let's take a break. Use this quiet lamp to write
your facts. **Do you feel a little better?**

What is it, Joey?

Do I see a flappy stim of joy?

Yes! I'm so glad that the noise is gone and I took a break! **I feel great!**

I was able to finish writing and make you a **surprise**.

I know you like when I help you, but puzzle pieces aren't for me.
I hope you're not mad, but here's what I made instead...

A Pegasus?

I love it!

I knew you would! They're on all your toys, books, and drawings! We can share this Pegasus.With your puzzle pieces, it belongs to both of us.

Even though we are different, we can always help each other.

Now let's go play!

Magnifying Glass Explanations

Page 3 - All the things you hear, touch, taste, smell, and see are called **sensory input**. Each person experiences sensory input differently.

Neurodivergent people like Joey often cannot "tune out" sensory input like their neurotypical peers can. Joey's ears work as well as his neurotypical sister's, but his brain cannot ignore input that he sees, smells, hears, tastes, or feels. Sometimes sensory input can be so overwhelming it causes intense feelings like distress or pure joy.

Pages 4 and 5 - People can be sensory seeking, sensory avoidant, or both! Knowing your own unique sensory needs is very helpful.

There are many tools like noise-canceling headphones, chewelry, fidget spinners, putty, and gum to help people stim. There are many different ways to stim because everyone has different needs. Do you ever use tools to help you stim or soothe your senses?

Page 6 and 7 -People like a good friend or relative often recognize the difference between happy and distressed stims. If you don't know the person very well, let them stim as long as it's safe. It's important!

Magnifying Glass Explanations

Page 8 - Not everyone stims. Do you ever stim?

Page 11 - If a person is unable to manage their sensory input, it can be overwhelming and lead to **burnout** or a **meltdown**. When sensory overload happens, a person may be unable to use words to ask for help. If

someone is stimming when they're upset, it's best to find ways to comfort the individual or remove the stressor. Always give the person stimming time to process the feeling. You can talk about it later, after they've recovered.

Page 20 - Some lights hum or buzz as they operate, especially when an appliance is in use at the same time. The sound produced can feel like torture to people sensitive to sounds. This is just one example of how sensory input can deeply affect one person, but might not be an issue to another.

Feelings

Naming your feelings accurately is important to understanding your current mindset. If you want to understand yourself, it's important to call a feeling by its proper name. Feelings are neither right nor wrong, and they never last forever. It's critical to feel the feeling completely, even if it's an upset feeling. Take time to name whatever you feel, and then think about why you might feel that way.

ANGER

Aggravated	Irritated, Vexed
Annoyed	Displeased, Exasperated
Betrayed	Failed, Cheated
Bitter	Resentful
Critical	Negative feelings to someone else's actions or your own
Frustrated	Defeated/unable to attain desire
Furious	Enraged, Outraged
Hostile	Aggressive, Warlike
Humiliated	Embarrassed, Judged
Mad	Furious
Violated	Disobeyed, Double-crossed, Wronged

DISCONNECTED

Apathetic	Uninterested
Bored	Indifferent, Detached
Busy	Overly preoccupied
Confused	In a fog, Bewildered, Perplexed
Rushed	Hurried
Sleepy	Sluggish, Drowsy
Stressed	Burdened
Tired	Fatigued, Drained
Unfocused	Unable to concentrate

HAPPY

Accepted	Believed, Understood, Welcomed
Amazed	Perplexed, Stunned
Content	Untroubled, At peace
Curious	Full of questions or wonder, Interested
Empowered	Full of ability and/or strength
Excited	Enthusiastic, Eager
Peaceful	Relaxed, Calm
Playful	Joyful, High-spirited
Sensitive	Perceptive, Aware
Thrilled	Excited, Exhilarated
Trusting	Unguarded

Feelings

Use this page to help name your feelings accurately. These are just a few feelings and the definitions aren't all listed. If you reflect on your feelings, you may notice patterns of when, why, and how particular feelings emerge and it could help you understand yourself better.

DISGUST

Awful	Unpleasant, Very bad
Detestable	Despicable, Obnoxious
Disapproving	Critical, Scathing
Disappointed	Let down, Saddened
Embarrassed	Awkward, Unaccepted, Uncomfortable
Hesitant	Uncertain, Doubtful
Horrified	Terrorized, Shocked
Judgmental	Deciding if others' actions are good/bad
Nauseated	Sickened (literally or figuratively)
Numb	Unfeeling
Revolted	Shocked, Horrified, Repelled

SAD

Abandoned	Rejected, Stranded
Ashamed	Sorry, Full of remorse
Despair	Distressed, Miserable
Disappointed	Upset, Crestfallen
Depressed	Low, Upset, Unhappy
Embarrassed	Awkward, Unaccepted, Uneasy
Empty	Without energy, Worthless
Grief	Full of sadness for a loss
Guilty	Blameworthy, Responsible for something bad
Hurt	Injured literally or figuratively
Lonely	Isolated
Remorseful	Sorry, Regretful
Victimized	Cheated, Tricked, wronged
Vulnerable	Unprotected, Unsafe

FEARFUL

Anxious	Worried, Concerned
Excluded	Left out
Exposed	Open to criticism, Vulnerable
Frightened	Scared
Helpless	Weak, Vulnerable
Inadequate	Not good enough
Insecure	Not feeling safe
Nervous	Tense, Unsure
Overwhelmed	Devastated
Persecuted	Punished unfairly, Victimized
Rejected	Deemed inadequate/ not good enough/ misunderstood
Threatened	Intimidated, Under attack
Weak	Frail, Sickly, Without strength
Withdrawn	Silent, Distant, Reserved
Worried	Disturbed, Troubled

Overwhelming Situations

 **Burnout** A state of emotional, physical, and/or mental exhaustion caused by excessive and/or prolonged stress. Burnout prevents a person from accomplishing desired goals and/or necessary tasks. It occurs when a person feels overwhelmed, emotionally drained, and/or unable to meet constant demands. The causes of burnout will vary due to many factors like one's sensory needs, lifestyle, and support system. To prevent burnout, it's important to take time to rest and recharge after doing something demanding.

 **Meltdown** An intense response to overwhelming circumstances—a complete loss of behavioral control. A meltdown is an involuntary coping mechanism after one's system(s) become(s) overwhelmed with sensory input and/or other stressors. Stimming can help prevent meltdowns.

If you want to be an ally to someone experiencing the distress of a meltdown, give the person privacy, a safe place, and never film him/her/them. Let it pass and don't have them explain the situation as it is happening. Talking may be an option after there's been enough time to rest and recover, if the person is willing and able.

A meltdown is not the same thing as a tantrum and these terms should never be used interchangeably.

 **Tantrum** In contrast to a meltdown, is a conscious, voluntary behavior done for the purpose of manipulating another to get a specific reward. Though they might sometimes look similar, knowing the difference between a tantrum and meltdown is crucial to appropriately help people with their unique needs.

 **Regulation** Managing sensory input in a way that helps a person live a happy and healthy life and prevent burnout/meltdowns. Everyone has a unique way to regulate/realign/ ground themselves. There are a variety of ways to regulate one's body, including stimming, but others are listed on the next page.

Coping Effectively

Sit down

Rest.

Breathe

Put one hand over your heart and one hand over your belly.

Remember

You're not in an emergency and slowing down is ok!

Connect

Focus on your senses and try to name things you can smell, taste, see, touch, and/or hear.

Count

Going backwards or forwards in multiples is a way to refocus your mind.

Honor

Acknowledge how you are feeling and that you are an amazing person!

Neurotypes

Neurology The way a brain operates/is wired to interpret the world. All people are born with a specific neurology/neurotype.

Neurotypical (NT) The neurotype of people who aren't neurodivergent.

Neurodivergent (ND) The neurotype of people who aren't neurotypical. This term is often used for autistic people, but can also be used for others who aren't autistic, but still neurodivergent. ND refers to unique variation in the way the brain processes information compared to neurotypical processing.

Allistic A person who is not autistic. Allistic people can be neurodivergent, like a person with ADHD or dyslexia.

Autism A neurological difference compared to neurotypical brains that affects the way people sense the world, think, communicate, and move. Autism is based on a spectrum.

Many people prefer the term "autistic" instead of "having autism" or "person with autism". This is because it describes one's neurology, which affects every part of life. "Having autism" can make one's neurology sound like an accessory that can be added or taken away when needed, which of course is impossible. If you're unsure how to discuss autism, the best choice is to listen to individuals who are on the spectrum about the language they prefer.

Everyone has some autistic traits because autistic traits are human traits. But we are not all autistic so it would be harmful and wrong to suggest that.

The infinity symbol is the most preferred symbol of autistic people. Rainbow colors are also often used to depict the autism spectrum. Find out more at sensationalstims.com or on Facebook and Instagram @sensationalstims.

About the Author and Illustrator

Erin Garcia is an allistic public educator and writer in California where she lives with her family. Her maiden name is Dieterle (Dee-ter-lee) which roughly translates from German to "little warrior of the people". She co-authored Tiger Livy and founded Infinite Inclusion Inc., a nonprofit dedicated to making life more inclusive through art. Erin's mission is to create enthusiastic allies who cultivate empathy in their communities. The Case of Sensational Stims was inspired by this ideal. Learn more about what else Erin is up to at eringarciabooks.com.

Christian Bajusz (pronounced Bay-ihs) is an artist on the autism spectrum who lives in Virginia. His last name means "mustache" in Hungarian. When he was seven, he taught himself how to draw by studying classic cartoons like Mickey Mouse and Popeye, and has been working hard ever since. He dreams of having his own cartoon series one day. When he's not drawing, Christian enjoys researching and creating archives of old TV broadcasts. If you want to see his latest work, find him on Twitter @CDCBsVCR.

CPSIA information can be obtained
at www.ICGtesting.com
Printed in the USA
LVHW071029100622
720957LV00008B/83